Copyright 2009, Gooseberry Patch
Second Printing, May, 2011

All rights reserved. No part of this book may be reproduced or utilized in any form or by any means, electronic or mechanical, including photocopying and recording, or by any information storage and retrieval system, without permission in writing from the publisher. Printed in Korea.

An old-fashioned stoneware butter crock makes a festive fall centerpiece when filled with Indian corn and dried flowers.

Sweet Pumpkin Dip

Makes 9 cups

2 8-oz. pkgs. cream cheese, softened
4 c. powdered sugar
30-oz. can pumpkin pie filling mix
2 t. cinnamon
1 t. ground ginger
gingersnap cookies

Mix cream cheese and powdered sugar in a large bowl. Blend in pie filling and spices; cover and chill. Serve with gingersnaps for dipping.

Create your own hay maze...it's simple. Stack bales of hay or straw and make a little path that runs through them. The kids will laugh all the way through it!

Touchdown Pinwheels

Makes 40 servings

2 green onions, chopped
8-oz. pkg. cream cheese, softened
1-oz. pkg. ranch salad dressing mix
5 12-inch flour tortillas
3/4 c. pimento-stuffed olives, chopped
3/4 c. black olives, chopped
4-1/2 oz. can chopped green chiles, drained
4-oz. jar chopped pimentos, drained
Garnish: fresh parsley, chopped

Combine first 3 ingredients; spread evenly over one side of each tortilla. Stir remaining ingredients together; spoon over cream cheese mixture. Roll up each tortilla jelly-roll style; wrap each in plastic wrap. Refrigerate for at least 2 hours; cut into one-inch slices and garnish with parsley.

Set mini pumpkins on top of terra cotta flower pots...
line them up the front porch steps for a cheery welcome

Apple-Cheese Fondue

Makes 4 servings

1 clove garlic, minced
1 c. dry white wine or apple juice
1/2 lb. Gruyère cheese, shredded
1/2 lb. Swiss cheese, diced
2 T. cornstarch
1/8 t. nutmeg
1/8 t. pepper
1 French baguette, torn into bite-size pieces
2 apples, cored, quartered and sliced

In a fondue pot or saucepan over medium heat, combine all ingredients except bread and apples. Bring to a simmer, stirring constantly, until cheese is melted. Serve with baguette and apple pieces for dipping.

Fill autumn windowboxes with straw, gourds, mini pumpkins and Indian corn.

Harvest Trail Mix

Makes about 3 pounds

10.5-oz. box bite-size crispy honey nut corn & rice cereal squares
8-oz. pkg. candy-coated chocolates
8-oz. bag candy corn
9-oz. pkg. raisins
12-oz. jar dry-roasted peanuts

Mix all ingredients together; store in an airtight container.

Enjoy yummy snacks outside. Light tables with tealights placed in hollowed-out apples, arrange hay bales for casual seating and fill sap buckets with sprays of bittersweet.

Apple Friendship Drink

Makes 2 servings

1 banana, peeled and sliced
1 apple, cored, peeled and cubed
4 strawberries, hulled
1 vanilla bean
2 T. honey
1/8 t. cardamom
1/2 c. apple cider

Place banana, apple and strawberries in a blender; set aside. Slice vanilla bean in half; scrape one side onto a spoon, discarding shell. Add vanilla seed spoonful to blender, reserving remaining half of vanilla bean for use in another recipe. Pour in honey and cardamom; purée mixture. Gradually blend in cider; pour into cups to serve.

On a cool evening, invite friends over to enjoy a crackling fire, warm cider and favorite movie.

Hot Caramel Apple Cider

Makes 32 servings

1 gal. apple cider
1 pkg. mulling spices
12-oz. jar caramel ice cream topping
1 c. whipping cream
2 to 3 t. sugar
1/2 t. vanilla extract
Garnish: cinnamon sticks, ground cinnamon

Heat cider and mulling spices as directed on spice package. When thoroughly heated, pour into individual cups and top with one teaspoon caramel topping; stir to dissolve. Place whipping cream and sugar in a bowl; add vanilla. Using an electric mixer, blend until soft peaks form. Add a dollop to each mug of cider; garnish with a cinnamon stick and a sprinkle of cinnamon.

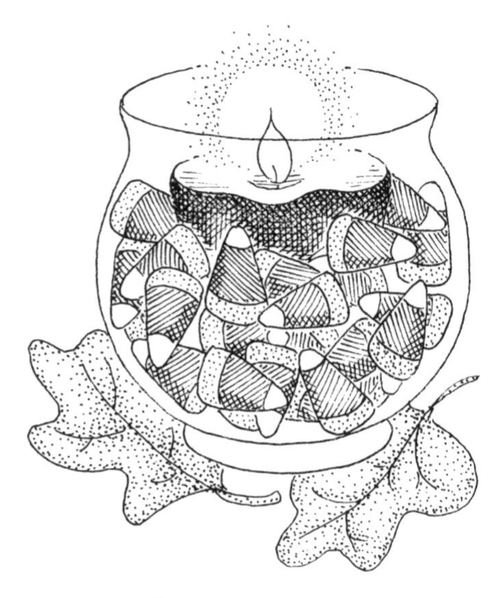

Fill vintage jelly jars with candy corn and set a tealight inside each one. Their sweet glow will make the prettiest place settings!

Autumn Pancakes

Makes 6 servings

1/2 c. quick-cooking oats, uncooked
1-1/2 c. boiling water
1-1/2 c. all-purpose flour
2 t. baking powder
1/8 t. salt
3 T. sugar
1/2 t. cinnamon
1 egg, beaten
1 c. milk
1 apple, cored, peeled and coarsely chopped
1/4 c. chopped walnuts
3 T. butter, melted
Garnish: maple syrup or powdered sugar

Place oats in a small bowl. Pour boiling water over oats and let stand 5 minutes; set aside. Combine flour, baking powder, salt, sugar and cinnamon in a large bowl. Add oat mixture, egg, milk, apple, nuts and melted butter; mix well. Pour batter by 1/4 cupfuls into a lightly greased skillet over medium-high heat. Cook until bubbles appear on the surface, about 2 minutes. Turn pancakes over and cook until golden, about one minute longer. Garnish with syrup or powdered sugar.

When the weather turns cool, guest rooms need special touches...an extra quilt at the foot of the bed and flannel sheets to snuggle into.

Pumpkin Waffles

Makes 6 servings

2 c. all-purpose flour
2 T. baking powder
1 T. cinnamon
1/2 t. coriander
1/2 t. nutmeg
1/4 t. salt
4 eggs, separated
1-1/2 c. milk
1 c. canned pumpkin
3/4 c. butter, melted
1 T. vanilla extract
Garnish: butter, maple syrup

Combine flour, baking powder, spices and salt in a large mixing bowl; set aside. In a second bowl, beat egg yolks slightly; blend in milk, pumpkin, butter and vanilla. Add pumpkin mixture to flour mixture, stirring until just combined. In a small bowl, beat egg whites until stiff peaks form; gently fold into pumpkin mixture. Pour one to 1-1/2 cups batter onto a preheated, lightly greased waffle iron. Bake according to manufacturer's instructions. Repeat with remaining batter.

Top waffles with yummy Blueberry-Honey Butter. In a food processor, blend one pound unsalted butter, slightly softened, with one pint ripe blueberries and 1/4 cup honey until smooth.

Breakfast Apple Cobbler

Makes 6 to 8 servings

8 apples, cored, peeled and sliced
1/4 c. sugar
1/8 t. cinnamon
juice of 1 lemon
1/4 c. butter, melted
2 c. granola

Combine all ingredients in a slow cooker. Cover; cook on low setting for 7 to 9 hours, or on high setting for 2 to 3 hours.

Sweet breads make yummy sandwiches.
Top slices of pumpkin bread with peanut butter, jam, flavored cream cheese or apple slices.

Chocolate Chippy Pumpkin Bread *Makes 2 loaves*

3 c. all-purpose flour
1 t. baking soda
1 t. salt
2 t. cinnamon
4 eggs
2 c. sugar
15-oz. can pumpkin
1-1/4 c. oil
1-1/2 c. semi-sweet
1-1/2 c. chocolate chips

Combine flour, baking soda, salt and cinnamon in a large bowl; set aside. Beat together eggs, sugar, pumpkin and oil in a large bowl; stir into dry ingredients just until moistened. Fold in chocolate chips; pour into two, greased 8"x4" loaf pans. Bake at 350 degrees for 60 to 70 minutes, or until a toothpick tests clean. Cool for 10 minutes before removing to wire racks to finish cooling.

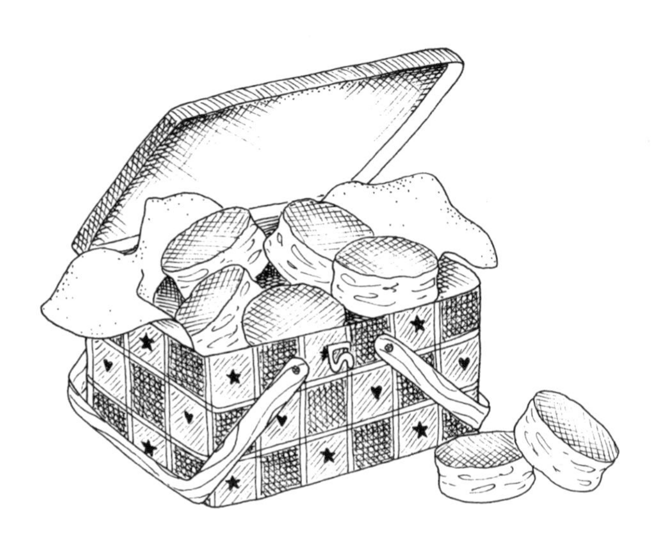

Add a yummy touch to homemade biscuits... brush each with butter, then sprinkle with dried parsley or rosemary before baking.

Sweet Potato Biscuits

Makes 2 dozen

2 c. all-purpose flour
2/3 c. sugar
2 T. baking powder
1-1/2 t. salt
1/2 c. shortening
2 c. sweet potatoes, cooked, peeled and mashed
1/4 c. buttermilk

Sift flour, sugar, baking powder and salt together; cut in shortening. Mix in potatoes and buttermilk; turn out onto a lightly floured board. Knead lightly; roll out 1/2-inch thick. Cut with a biscuit cutter; arrange on greased baking sheets. Bake at 475 degrees for 12 to 15 minutes.

A quick & easy seasoning mix is six parts salt to one part pepper. Keep it close to the stove in a large shaker... so handy when seasoning pork chops or chicken.

Autumn Apple Pork Chops

Makes 4 servings

4 pork chops
3/4 c. barbecue sauce
3/4 c. apple juice

Brown pork chops in a 12" skillet until done. Mix barbecue sauce and apple juice together; pour over pork chops. Reduce heat; simmer until liquid reduces, about 20 minutes.

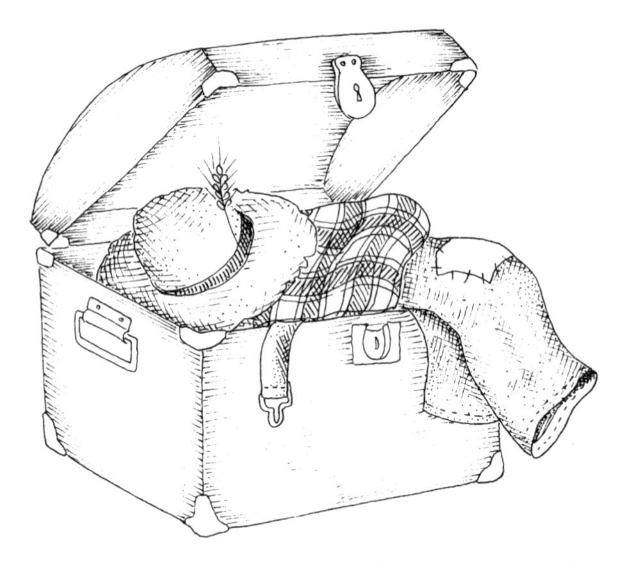

An old trunk is ideal for filling with dress-up clothes for scarecrow-making. Have a best-dressed scarecrow contest while dinner's cooking!

Gobbler Bake

Makes 4 to 6 servings

3 c. prepared stuffing
2-3/4 oz. can French fried onions, divided
10-3/4 oz. can cream of celery soup
3/4 c. milk
1-1/2 c. cooked turkey, cubed
10-oz. pkg. frozen green peas, thawed

Combine stuffing and half of onions. Spoon mixture into a lightly greased 9"x9" baking pan, pressing it into bottom and up sides of pan. Blend remaining ingredients; pour over stuffing. Bake, covered, at 350 degrees for 30 minutes. Uncover; top with remaining onions. Bake for an additional 5 minutes.

For a new twist, substitute packaged stuffing mix for bread crumbs in meatball or meatloaf recipes.

Homestyle Meatloaf

Makes 6 to 8 servings

2 lbs. ground beef
1 egg, beaten
3/4 c. catsup
1/4 c. milk
1 onion, chopped
1 c. pretzels, crushed
Garnish: catsup

Combine all ingredients except garnish; mix well. Place in a greased 9"x5" loaf pan. Bake at 350 degrees for one hour; top with additional catsup during last 15 minutes.

How about a game of pumpkin bowling? Simply roll pumpkins toward 2-liter bottles filled with water!

Maple-Glazed Turkey

Makes 10 to 12 servings

12-lb. turkey, giblet package removed and reserved for use in another recipe
optional: favorite stuffing
4 T. butter, melted and divided
salt and pepper to taste
1 T. fresh sage, minced
1 T. fresh marjoram, minced
2 T. fresh parsley, minced
3-1/2 c. chicken broth
3 T. maple syrup
1/8 t. ground ginger

Pat turkey dry; loosely stuff if desired. Place in a large roasting pan; loosely tie legs together with kitchen string. Brush turkey with 2 tablespoons melted butter and sprinkle generously with salt and pepper. Insert meat thermometer into thickest part of thigh without touching bone. Mix together sage, marjoram and parsley; loosen skin on turkey's breast and spoon half of the herb mixture under the skin. Place 1/2 cup of broth in the roasting pan. Roast for 2-1/2 hours at 325 degrees, basting every half hour with an additional 1/2 cup of broth and pan juices. Blend the remaining butter, remaining herbs, maple syrup and ginger in a small bowl; brush turkey with mixture. Continue roasting an additional 30 minutes or until meat thermometer reads 165 degrees. Allow turkey to stand about 15 minutes before slicing.

Paint names on colorful mini gourds for whimsical placecards.

Cranberry Chicken

Makes 4 to 6 servings

2 T. oil
4 to 6 boneless, skinless
chicken breasts
1 onion, sliced
1/2 c. catsup
8-oz. can whole-berry
cranberry sauce
2 T. brown sugar, packed
1 T. Worcestershire sauce

Heat oil in a large skillet over medium heat; add chicken and cook until golden on both sides. Remove chicken to a lightly greased 13"x9" baking pan. Add onion to skillet; sauté until tender, about 3 to 5 minutes. Stir in remaining ingredients; heat through. Pour mixture over chicken; bake, uncovered, at 350 degrees for 20 to 25 minutes.

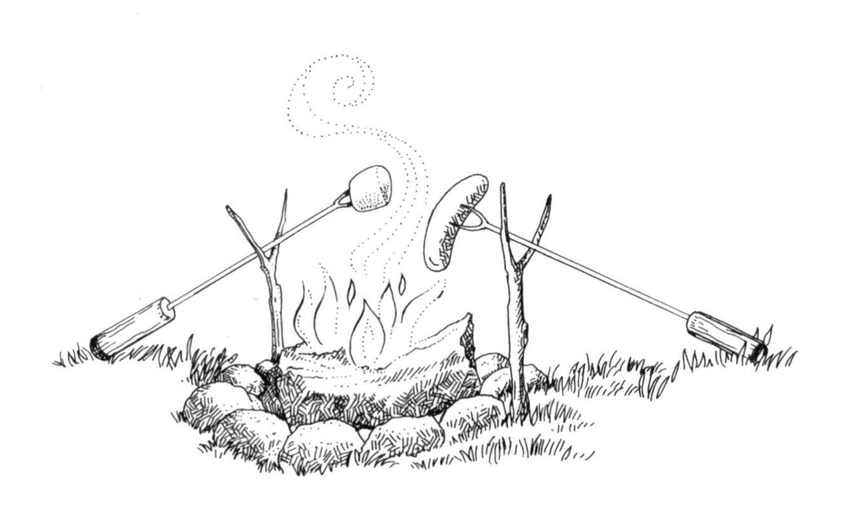

Tuck aluminum foil-wrapped sweet potatoes into campfire coals for a treat. When they're tender, sprinkle with brown sugar and butter, then eat right from the foil package.

Farmhouse Pork & Sauerkraut

Makes 6 servings

4-lb. pork loin roast
1 T. oil
29-oz. can sauerkraut, drained and rinsed
1/4 c. water
1 onion, sliced
1 potato, peeled and sliced
10-3/4 oz. can Cheddar cheese soup
1 T. caraway seed
1 Granny Smith apple, cored, peeled and sliced
salt and pepper to taste

In a skillet over medium heat, brown pork in oil on all sides; place in a slow cooker. Combine remaining ingredients except salt and pepper in a large bowl. Pour over roast; cover and cook on low setting for 10 hours. Season with salt and pepper before serving.

Bales of hay make comfy seating for a casual fall cookout.

Fresh Tomato Pie

Makes 8 servings

1 c. mayonnaise
1 c. grated Parmesan cheese
3 to 4 tomatoes, peeled and sliced
9-inch deep-dish pie crust, baked
6 to 8 slices bacon, crisply cooked and crumbled
salt and pepper to taste

Blend mayonnaise and Parmesan cheese together; set aside. Layer half the tomatoes into the pie crust, sprinkle with bacon. Add remaining tomatoes; salt and pepper to taste. Spread mayonnaise mixture on top, spreading to edges. Bake at 400 degrees for 15 to 17 minutes, or until top is lightly golden.

A centerpiece in a snap...nestle a plump candle in the center of a simple glass salad or punch bowl, then fill around it with small apples.

Harvest Home Roast Turkey *Makes 10 to 12 servings*

14 to 15-lb. turkey, thawed
2 cloves garlic, halved and divided
1 t. seasoning salt, divided
1 onion, quartered
1 bunch fresh parsley
2 sprigs fresh thyme
5 to 6 leaves fresh sage
2 T. olive oil
pepper to taste

Pat turkey dry. Remove giblets and neck; reserve for another use. Rub inside of turkey with one clove garlic and 1/2 teaspoon salt; stuff with remaining garlic, onion and herbs. Place turkey breast-side up on a rack in a large roaster pan. Brush oil over turkey; sprinkle with remaining salt and pepper to taste. Roast turkey at 325 degrees about 2-3/4 to 3 hours, basting occasionally with pan drippings, until a meat thermometer inserted into thickest part of thigh registers 165 degrees. If needed, tent turkey with aluminum foil to prevent browning too quickly. Let turkey stand 15 to 20 minutes before carving; discard garlic, onion and herbs.

Nippy fall evenings are a fine time for a backyard cookout.
Hang lanterns on the fence and in the trees
for twinkling light...magical!

Brown Sugar Short Ribs

Makes 4 servings

2 T. oil
3 to 5 lbs. short ribs
1 T. garlic, minced
1 c. brown sugar, packed
1/2 c. catsup
1/2 c. soy sauce
1/4 c. white vinegar
1 c. water
1 t. salt

Heat oil in a stockpot; add ribs and garlic. Sauté until ribs are browned. Mix remaining ingredients together in small mixing bowl; pour over ribs. Bring to a boil; reduce heat and simmer for one hour.

Serve tummy-warming stews in edible mini pumpkins. Cut tops off pumpkins, scoop out seeds and brush lightly with oil. Bake on a baking sheet at 350 degrees for 30 to 40 minutes, until tender. Ladle in hot stew...yum!

Pumpkin Patch Stew

Makes 6 to 8 servings

1 onion, finely chopped
1 clove garlic, minced
1 T. dried basil
1 T. olive oil
2 lbs. pork tenderloin, cubed
28-oz. can diced tomatoes
15-oz. can pumpkin
14-1/2 oz. can chicken broth
1/2 c. white wine or chicken broth
1/2 t. salt
1/4 t. pepper
4 potatoes, peeled and cubed
1/2 lb. green beans, cut into 1-inch pieces
4-inch cinnamon stick

In a stockpot over medium heat, sauté onion, garlic and basil in oil until onion is tender, one to 2 minutes. Add pork; cook for 3 to 4 minutes, until lightly browned. Stir in tomatoes with juice, pumpkin, broth, wine or broth, salt and pepper; bring to a boil. Reduce heat to low; cook, stirring occasionally, for 10 minutes. Add remaining ingredients. Cover; simmer for one hour, or until potatoes are tender. Discard cinnamon stick.

In late October or early November, plant flowering bulbs for springtime color...it's the ideal time.

Tangy Turkey Salad Croissants

Makes 6 servings

2 c. cooked turkey breast, cubed
1/2 c. cranberries, finely chopped
1 orange, peeled and chopped
1/2 c. mayonnaise
1 t. mustard
1 t. sugar
1/2 t. salt
1/4 c. chopped pecans
6 croissants, split
Garnish: lettuce leaves

In a large bowl, combine turkey, cranberries, orange, mayonnaise, mustard, sugar and salt; chill. Just before serving, stir in pecans. Top each croissant with 1/2 cup turkey mixture and a lettuce leaf.

Everybody loves a tailgating party...and a small-town college rivalry can be just as much fun as a Big Ten game. Load up a pickup truck with tasty finger foods, sandwich fixin's and a big washtub full of bottled drinks on ice.

Tailgate Party Sandwiches *Makes 20 to 24 servings*

1 onion, chopped
1/2 c. margarine, softened
2 T. poppy seed
1 T. mustard
1 T. Worcestershire sauce
20 to 24 dinner rolls, halved
1 lb. baked ham, shaved
8-oz pkg. sliced Swiss cheese

Mix onion, margarine, poppy seed, mustard and Worcestershire sauce together; spread mixture on both sides of rolls. Cover one side with ham; place cheese over top. Replace top of roll; arrange on ungreased baking sheets. Bake at 400 degrees for 25 to 30 minutes or until cheese is melted; separate rolls before serving.

Plan a fall family outing to a farm. Many are open to the public for good old-fashioned fun like corn mazes, hayrides and pumpkin picking. You'll enjoy it as much as the kids!

Mom's Sloppy Joes

Makes 8 to 10 servings

1 lb. ground beef
1/2 c. onion, chopped
1/2 c. celery, thinly sliced
1-1/2 c. catsup
1/4 c. brown sugar, packed
1 T. vinegar
1-1/2 T. mustard
salt and pepper to taste
8 to 10 sandwich buns

Brown beef with onion and celery in a 12" skillet; drain and set aside. Mix remaining ingredients except for the buns together; add to beef mixture. Bring to a boil; reduce heat and simmer until thoroughly warmed. Spoon onto buns to serve.

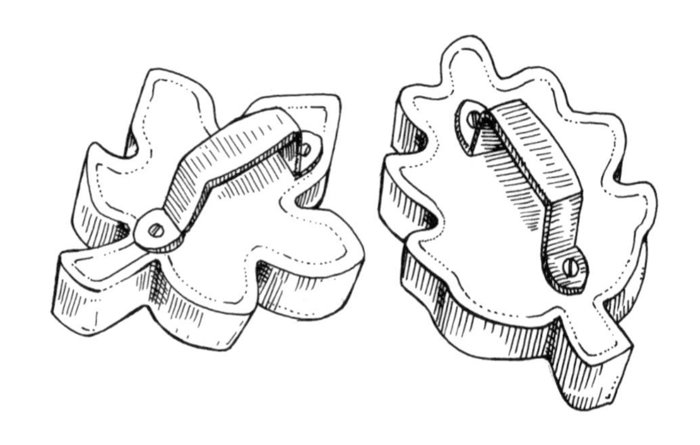

Serve up savory soups with leaf-shaped toast created by simply using a cookie cutter on toast slices.

Bacon-Corn Chowder

Makes 4 to 6 servings

5 c. redskin potatoes, cubed
16-oz. pkg. frozen corn
6 slices bacon, crisply cooked and crumbled
1/4 c. dried, minced onion
2 14-1/2 oz. cans chicken broth
1 c. water
2 t. garlic salt
1 t. pepper
1/4 t. turmeric
12-oz. can evaporated milk
8-oz. pkg. shredded Monterey Jack cheese
Optional: fresh chives, chopped

Combine all ingredients except milk, cheese and chives in a slow cooker. Cover; cook on low setting for 8 to 9 hours, or until potatoes are tender. Stir in milk and cheese; cover until cheese melts. Garnish with chives, if desired.

An autumn soup supper is a wonderfully easy way to get together with friends & neighbors. Each family brings a pot of a favorite homemade soup...you supply go-withs like rolls, cider and a yummy dessert.

Auction Chili

Makes 4 to 6 servings

1 lb. ground beef
1 onion, chopped
1 t. oil
15-oz. can diced tomatoes
10-3/4 oz. can tomato soup
15-oz. can kidney beans, drained
salt to taste
1/8 t. pepper
1/4 t. dried cumin
1/2 t. chili powder

Brown ground beef and onion together in oil; drain. Add remaining ingredients; heat until warmed through.

Spend the day at a barn auction. Look for cast-offs that can be put to new use...you never know what you'll find!

Sweet Cornbread

Makes 8 to 10 servings

1 c. yellow cornmeal
2 c. all-purpose flour
1 T. baking powder
1/2 t. salt
1 c. sugar
4 eggs, separated
1 c. half-and-half
1 t. vanilla extract
3/4 c. butter, melted

Combine cornmeal, flour, baking powder, salt and sugar in a medium bowl; set aside. Mix together egg yolks, half-and-half, vanilla and melted butter in a separate bowl; add to dry ingredients and stir until thoroughly moistened. Beat egg whites until stiff; gently fold into batter. Pour into a greased 13"x9" baking pan; bake at 350 degrees for 30 minutes, or until toothpick tests clean.

Pick up some sturdy vintage mugs at tag sales for serving steamy soups & stews.. They hold the heat well... wonderful to wrap chilly fingers around!

Curried Pumpkin Soup

Makes 6 servings

16-oz. pkg. sliced mushrooms
1/2 c. onion, chopped
2 T. butter
2 T. all-purpose flour
1 T. curry powder
3 c. chicken or vegetable broth
15-oz. can pumpkin
1 T. honey
1/8 t. nutmeg
salt and pepper to taste
1 c. whipping cream or
evaporated milk
Garnish: sour cream, croutons

Sauté mushrooms and onion with butter in a large saucepan over medium heat until softened. Add flour and curry powder; cook over medium heat for 5 minutes, stirring constantly. Add broth, pumpkin, honey, nutmeg, salt and pepper to taste. Simmer for 15 minutes, stirring occasionally. Stir in cream or milk; heat through without boiling. Serve with a dollop of sour cream & croutons.

Spend the weekend at a country cabin. Go leaf peeping, hike in the woods and enjoy the brisk air!

October Bisque

Makes 8 servings

1 onion, chopped
1/4 c. butter
4 c. chicken broth
28-oz. can whole tomatoes
1 T. sugar
2 15-oz. cans pumpkin
2 T. fresh parsley, chopped
2 T. fresh chives, chopped

Sauté onion in butter until onion is tender. Add broth and simmer for 15 minutes. Place tomatoes in a blender or food processor and blend until smooth. Add tomato mixture, sugar, pumpkin, parsley and chives to broth; heat through.

For the tenderest muffins, don't overmix...just stir the batter until moistened. A few lumps won't matter.

Sweet Potato Cranberry Muffins *Makes one dozen*

1-1/2 c. all-purpose flour
1/2 c. sugar
2 t. baking powder
3/4 t. salt
1/2 t. cinnamon
1/2 t. nutmeg
1 egg, beaten
1/2 c. milk
1/2 c. mashed sweet potatoes
1/4 c. butter, melted
1 c. cranberries, chopped
cinnamon-sugar to taste

Combine flour, sugar, baking powder, salt and spices in a large bowl; set aside. In a separate bowl, combine egg, milk, sweet potatoes and butter; stir into flour mixture just until moistened. Fold in cranberries. Fill paper-lined muffin cups 1/2 full; sprinkle with cinnamon-sugar. Bake at 375 degrees for 20 to 22 minutes, until a toothpick tests clean. Cool completely.

Carve or drill a pattern of round holes in hollowed-out pumpkins, then set tealights inside for a flickering glow.

Spicy Butternut Bake

Makes 4 servings

2 c. butternut squash, cooked and mashed
3 eggs, beaten
1 c. milk
1/4 c. butter, melted
3/4 c. sugar
1 t. ground ginger
1 t. cinnamon

Combine all ingredients in a large bowl; spread in a lightly greased 8"x8" baking pan. Bake at 350 degrees for 40 minutes; stir and return to oven. Bake for an additional 10 minutes.

Pull out Grandma's vintage casserole dishes...they're just right for baking hearty fall casseroles and desserts, with a side dish of nostalgia!

Brown Sugar Yams & Apples

Makes 8 servings

2 apples, cored, peeled and sliced
1/4 c. margarine
2-1/4 oz. pkg. chopped pecans
1/2 c. brown sugar, packed
1/2 t. cinnamon
3 15-oz. cans yams, drained
2 c. marshmallows

Place apples and margarine in a microwave-safe bowl; heat until apples are soft. Pour into an ungreased 13"x9" baking pan; mix in pecans, sugar, cinnamon and yams. Bake at 350 degrees for 35 to 40 minutes; sprinkle with marshmallows. Bake until marshmallows are golden.

Use bread bowls to serve up sides, salads or soups this harvest season. Simply hollow out a few small round loaves of bread and fill.

Feta & Walnut Salad

Makes 4 to 6 servings

5-oz. pkg. mixed salad greens
3/4 c. dried cranberries
1/2 c. crumbled feta cheese
1/2 c. chopped walnuts, toasted
2 T. balsamic vinegar
1 T. honey
1 t. Dijon mustard
1/4 c. olive oil

Toss greens, cranberries, feta cheese and walnuts together in a large bowl. In a small bowl, whisk vinegar, honey and mustard until well blended; gradually add oil, whisking until combined. Pour over salad and toss to coat.

How much dressing to fix when stuffing a turkey? Here's a simple rule of thumb...for every pound of turkey, figure on 1/2 cup of stuffing.

Mom's Sausage Dressing

Makes 8 to 10 servings

1/2 c. butter
2 stalks celery, chopped
1 onion, chopped
5 c. cornbread, crumbled
3 c. day-old white bread, cubed
1/2 T. poultry seasoning
1/2 T. dried sage
1 t. salt
1 t. pepper
1 lb. ground pork sausage, browned and drained
2 14-1/2 oz. cans chicken broth
10-3/4 oz. can cream of chicken soup
4 to 5 eggs, beaten

Melt butter in a skillet over medium heat. Add celery and onion; heat until tender and set aside. Mix together breads and seasonings in a large bowl. Add celery mixture, sausage, broth, soup, eggs and enough water to make mixture soupy; mix well. Spoon into a greased 13"x9" baking pan. Bake, uncovered, at 350 degrees for 30 to 40 minutes, or until golden and heated through.

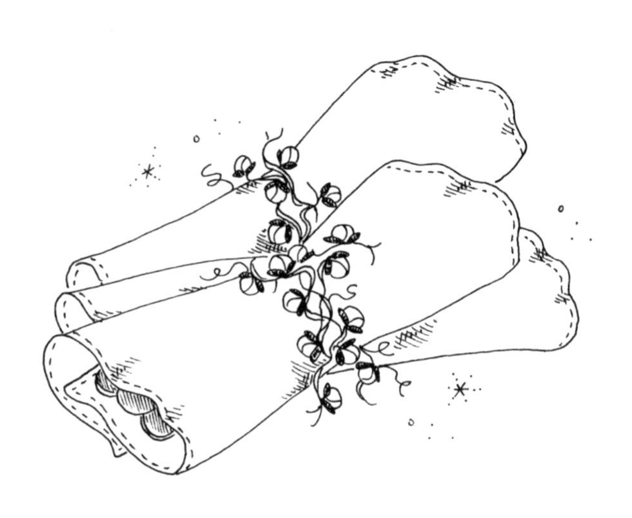

Roll up homespun napkins, tie with ribbon bows and slip a sprig of bittersweet under the ribbons...simple!

Aunt Mary's Cornbread Salad

Makes 12 to 15 servings

4 c. cornbread, crumbled
2 c. chicken, cooked and
 chopped
1 c. green onion, chopped
1 c. fresh parsley, chopped
1/2 c. green pepper, chopped
1/2 c. dill pickles, chopped
1/2 c. sliced water chestnuts
1 T. diced pimento
15-1/4 oz. can peas, drained
15-oz. can shoepeg corn,
 drained
1-1/2 T. sugar
1 t. salt
1/2 t. pepper
1 t. poultry seasoning
1/4 t. cayenne pepper
1 c. mayonnaise
Garnish: paprika

Mix together all ingredients except paprika in a serving bowl, stirring in mayonnaise last. Cover and chill for several hours. Sprinkle with paprika before serving.

On your next fall picnic, gather the prettiest autumn leaves...
they'll look so pretty arranged under the glass
of a vintage serving tray.

Sweet & Sour Coleslaw

Makes 8 servings

2 t. garlic salt
1 T. paprika
1 t. celery salt
1/4 c. sugar
1 c. oil, divided
1/2 c. cider vinegar, divided
2 T. fresh parsley, chopped
1 onion, chopped
1 head cabbage, shredded

Place garlic salt, paprika, celery salt and sugar in a blender; gradually pour in 1/2 cup oil. Blend for 3 minutes; add one tablespoon vinegar, continuing to blend. Repeat adding oil and then vinegar until both are gone; blend in parsley and onion. Let set at room temperature for one hour; blend again. Pour over shredded cabbage; cover and refrigerate for 24 hours before serving.

Create a cheerful, harvest table runner. Lay sunflower blooms down the center of the table and surround with small, brightly colored gourds and pumpkins.

The Creamiest Mashed Potatoes *Makes 6 servings*

5 to 6 potatoes, peeled and cut into 1-inch cubes
3-oz. pkg. cream cheese, thinly sliced and softened
3 T. butter, softened
4 to 5 T. half-and-half or milk
2 cloves garlic, minced
salt and pepper to taste
2 T. fresh chives, snipped, or 3 T. dried chives
Garnish: additional butter

Cover potatoes with water in a large stockpot over medium-high heat. Boil potatoes until tender when pierced with a fork, about 15 minutes once they begin to boil. Drain; mash with either a hand masher or an electric mixer on medium speed. Add cream cheese, butter, half-and-half or milk, garlic, salt and pepper. Mix well until butter and cream cheese are melted. Fold in chives; top with a dollop or two of butter.

Small-town harvest festivals are full of old-fashioned fun... where else could you eat a pumpkin burger or cheer on an antique tractor pull? Check with your state's tourism office for a list of seasonal festivals and fairs in your area, then pick one and go!

Sauerbraten

Makes 6 to 8 servings

3 to 4-lb. bottom round pot roast
2 T. oil
2 onions, chopped
2 bay leaves
1/2 c. cider vinegar
1-1/2 c. water

Brown pot roast in oil in a large heavy pot with a lid. Add remaining ingredients; bring to a rolling boil, reduce heat and simmer 2 to 3 hours or until tender, turning meat about 4 times during cooking. Remove and discard bay leaves before serving.

For a really quick side dish, cook chopped green peppers in butter for about 5 minutes. Add canned corn and salt and simmer until golden...yummy.

Best Creamed Corn

Makes 4 servings

10-oz. pkg. frozen corn, thawed
1/2 c. whipping cream
1/2 c. milk
1/2 t. salt
1 T. sugar
1 T. margarine, melted
1 T. all-purpose flour

Combine the first 5 ingredients in a saucepan; bring to a boil. Reduce heat; stir occasionally. Whisk margarine with flour until smooth; add to corn mixture. Heat until thickened; stir constantly.

A leaf rubbing makes such a pretty bookmark. Place a leaf between 2 sheets of paper. Remove the wrapper from a crayon, turn the crayon on its side and gently rub over the top sheet of paper. Use decorative-edged scissors to trim.

Ham & Lima Bean Pot

Makes 4 to 6 servings

1-1/2 c. dried lima beans
6 c. water
1 c. cooked ham, diced
1 onion, chopped
1/3 c. molasses
1/3 c. chili sauce
1 T. vinegar
1 t. dry mustard
1/8 t. cayenne pepper

Combine beans and water in a stockpot; let stand overnight. Drain beans; add 6 cups fresh water. Simmer over low heat for 1-1/2 hours. Drain again, reserving one cup liquid. Combine cooked beans, reserved liquid and remaining ingredients. Mix well and spread in a lightly greased 2-quart casserole dish. Bake, uncovered, at 350 degrees for 30 minutes, or until golden.

A trip to the apple orchard will give you bushels of crisp, crunchy apples to share. Pass on a favorite apple recipe with a basket of fresh-picked apples.

Applesauce

Makes 4 to 6 servings

4 c. MacIntosh apples, cored, peeled and quartered
1 c. water
1/2 c. sugar
1 t. lemon juice
1/2 t. cinnamon
1/8 t. salt

Combine apples and water in a heavy saucepan; cook over low heat, covered, until apples are very soft. Remove from heat; stir in remaining ingredients. Serve warm or cold.

Soups & stews are so tasty served with warm bread. Top each slice with the prettiest butter pats...simply use a tiny cookie cutter to shape chilled butter slices.

Suzie-Q Candied Carrots

Makes 8 to 10 servings

2 lbs. carrots, peeled and sliced 1/4-inch thick
1/2 c. butter
1 c. brown sugar, packed
1/2 t. vanilla extract
1/2 t. pepper

Place carrots in a large saucepan; cover with water. Bring to a boil over medium-high heat. Cook until fork-tender; drain. Add butter, brown sugar, vanilla and pepper; simmer over medium heat until thickened, about 5 minutes.

Don't toss out that dab of leftover cranberry sauce! Purée it with balsamic vinaigrette to create a tangy salad dressing.

Spiced Cranberry Sauce

Makes 3-1/2 cups

1 c. water
1 c. brown sugar, packed
1/4 t. ground cloves
12-oz. pkg. cranberries
8-oz. can pineapple tidbits, drained
3/4 c. chopped pecans

Combine water, brown sugar, cloves and cranberries in a medium saucepan; bring to a boil over medium heat. Continue to boil until most cranberries pop, stirring often, about 7 to 10 minutes. Remove from heat; stir in pineapple and pecans.

Add a little autumn crunch to fall casseroles... sprinkle toasted pumpkin seeds on before popping the casserole dish into the oven.

Bacon-Topped Veggie Bake

Makes 4 to 6 servings

10-oz. pkg. frozen chopped broccoli
1 egg, beaten
14-3/4 oz. can creamed corn
1/4 c. margarine, melted
2 slices bread, toasted, buttered and cubed
3 slices bacon, crisply cooked and crumbled

Cook broccoli according to package directions; drain well. Combine with egg, corn and margarine. Mix well; place in a lightly greased 1-1/2 quart casserole dish. Bake, covered, at 350 degrees for 40 minutes. Top with cubed toast and crumbled bacon; bake, uncovered, an additional 20 minutes.

During the next autumn bonfire, enjoy a warm and tasty apple treat. Slide an apple on a metal skewer and roast until warmed throughout. Slice and spoon on caramel sauce or sprinkle with cinnamon & sugar.

Cinnamon Apples

Makes 8 servings

8 to 10 apples, cored, peeled and sliced
1/2 c. brown sugar, packed
1/2 c. sugar
1/4 c. butter
1/2 c. honey
1 t. vanilla extract
cinnamon to taste

Arrange apple slices in a 1-1/2 to 2-quart casserole dish; set aside. Heat sugars, butter and honey in a heavy saucepan until sugars dissolve; stir until bubbly. Remove from heat; stir in vanilla and set aside. Sprinkle apples with cinnamon; pour sugar mixture on top and stir gently until evenly coated. Cover with aluminum foil; bake at 400 degrees for 30 minutes or until apples are tender.

Warm up a chilly morning with a mug of chocolatey cocoa. Make it extra special by topping it off with a dollop of sweetened whipped cream. Beat together 1/2 pint whipping cream with one tablespoon sugar and one teaspoon vanilla until soft peaks form.

French Hot Chocolate

Makes 8 servings

2 to 3 1-oz. sqs. unsweetened baking chocolate
1/2 c. water
3/4 c. sugar
1/8 t. salt
1/2 c. whipping cream, whipped
6 c. hot milk

Melt chocolate in a double boiler over medium heat. Add water; stir constantly for 4 minutes. Add sugar and salt; cook 4 minutes longer, stirring constantly. Cool mixture; fold in whipped cream. To serve, place a heaping tablespoon of chocolate mixture into each serving cup and pour about one cup hot milk on top, or until cup is almost filled. Stir lightly to blend.

Whip up a big bowl of homemade caramel corn...
...terrific for snacking on during a favorite movie.

No-Fuss Caramel Corn

Makes about 12 cups

12 c. popped popcorn
Optional: 1-1/2 c. peanuts
1 c. brown sugar, packed
1/2 c. butter
1/4 c. light corn syrup
1/2 t. salt
1/2 t. baking soda

Place popcorn in a large brown paper bag; add peanuts, if using, and set aside. Combine brown sugar, butter, corn syrup and salt in a microwave-safe 2-quart glass bowl. Microwave on high setting for 3 to 4 minutes, stirring after each minute, until mixture comes to a boil. Microwave for 2 additional minutes without stirring. Stir in baking soda. Pour mixture over popcorn; close bag and shake well. Microwave in bag for 1-1/2 minutes. Shake bag well and pour into a roaster pan; cool and stir.

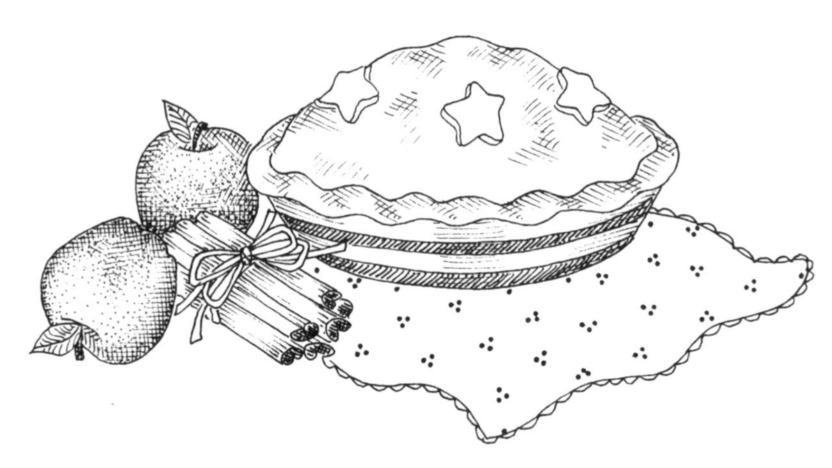

For a fun fall gathering, host a pie party and invite everyone to bring their best-loved pie and the recipe to share. You just might find a pie that becomes a new favorite.

Autumn Apple Pie

Makes 6 to 8 servings

6 Granny Smith apples, cored, peeled and thinly sliced
3 T. lemon juice
1/2 c. brown sugar, packed
1/2 c. plus 1 T. sugar, divided
2 t. cinnamon
1/4 t. nutmeg
3 T. all-purpose flour
1/4 c. butter, chilled and diced
9 caramels, unwrapped and quartered
2 9-inch pie crusts

Combine apples, lemon juice, brown sugar, 1/2 cup sugar, cinnamon, nutmeg, flour, butter and caramels. Stir until mixture evenly coats apples. Line a 9" pie plate with one pie crust; spoon filling into the crust. Cover with second crust; flute edges and vent as desired. Sprinkle remaining sugar over crust. Place on an aluminum foil-covered baking sheet. Bake at 375 degrees for 30 minutes; reduce heat to 350 degrees and bake an additional 20 minutes or until crust is golden.

Whip up cozy throws in bright red or russet plaid fleece...simply snip fringe all around the edges. They're so easy, you can make one for each member of the family in no time at all.

Cinnamon-Maple Nog

Makes 6 servings

6 c. milk
1 c. maple syrup
2 t. cinnamon
2 t. allspice
Optional: 6 4-inch cinnamon sticks

Combine milk and syrup in a saucepan; warm over medium-low heat, until heated through. Stir in cinnamon and allspice; serve hot. Garnish with cinnamon sticks, if desired.

Top off your pumpkin pie with cinnamon-spice whipped cream. In a chilled mixing bowl, beat 2 cups whipping cream, 1 tablespoon orange extract and 1/4 teaspoon cinnamon until stiff peaks form.

Frost on the Pumpkin Pie

Makes 8 servings

1/4 c. margarine, melted
1-1/2 c. gingersnap cookies, crushed
15-oz. can pumpkin
1 pt. vanilla ice cream, softened
1 c. powdered sugar
1 t. pumpkin pie spice
8-oz. container frozen whipped topping, thawed

Stir margarine and cookie crumbs together; press into an ungreased 9" pie plate. Refrigerate. Combine pumpkin, ice cream, powdered sugar and spice; blend until smooth. Fold in whipped topping; pour into crust. Freeze for several hours; let stand at room temperature for 20 to 25 minutes before serving.

Cookies are easy to wrap and tote to any autumn get-together...from a tailgating party to a picnic in the park.

Buttery Pecan Bars

Makes 25 servings

3 c. all-purpose flour
2 c. sugar, divided
1 c. butter
1/2 t. salt
4 eggs, beaten
1-1/2 c. corn syrup
3 T. butter, melted
1-1/2 t. vanilla extract
2-1/2 c. chopped pecans

Mix flour, 1/2 cup sugar, butter and salt together until mixture resembles crumbs; set aside. Press into a well-greased jelly-roll pan; bake at 350 degrees for 15 minutes. Combine eggs, corn syrup, melted butter, vanilla, pecans and remaining sugar until well blended; pour over hot crust. Return to oven for 25 additional minutes; cool and cut into bars.

A time-saving tip...fill plastic zipping bags with dry topping ingredients for a favorite fruit crisp or cobbler, then just add the wet ingredients later at baking time.

Colorado Pear Pie

Makes 6 servings

9-inch pie crust
1 c. plus 1 t. sugar, divided
2 T. cornstarch
1 T. cinnamon
5 c. pears, cored, peeled and thinly sliced
2 t. vanilla extract
1 egg white, beaten

On a lightly floured counter, roll out crust to a 16-inch circle, 1/8-inch thick. Transfer to an aluminum foil-lined baking sheet. Press out any creases; set aside. In a large bowl, combine one cup sugar, cornstarch and cinnamon. Add pears and vanilla; toss gently to coat. Spoon pears into center of crust, spreading them to within 2 inches of edge. Fold crust up over pears to form a border of about 2 inches, pleating and folding crust as needed. Brush folded edge with egg white and sprinkle with remaining sugar. Bake at 350 degrees until pears are tender and crust is lightly golden, about 20 minutes. Cool slightly on a wire rack before serving.

A touch of whimsy...use Mom's old cow-shaped milk pitcher to top desserts with cream.

Cinnamon Flop Cake

Makes 6 servings

1-1/2 c. sugar
2 T. butter, melted
1 egg
1 c. milk
2 c. all-purpose flour
2 t. baking powder
1/4 t. salt
1 c. brown sugar, packed
1/4 c. butter, chilled and diced
1-1/2 t. cinnamon

Place sugar, melted butter, egg and milk in a large mixing bowl; beat with an electric mixer on medium speed for 2 minutes. Stir in flour, baking powder and salt. Spread in a greased 8"x8" baking pan. Sprinkle with brown sugar; dot with diced butter and sprinkle with cinnamon. Bake at 425 degrees for about 35 minutes, until a toothpick inserted in center comes out clean. Cool 10 minutes; cut into squares. Serve warm.

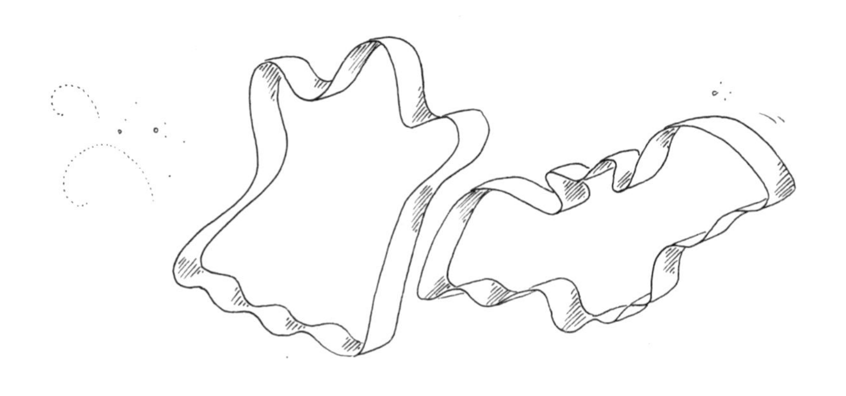

Mini cookie cutters are just the right size to make fudge cut-outs...try using leaf, ghost or pumpkin shapes.

Pumpkin Fudge

Makes about 6 1/2 dozen

5-oz. can evaporated milk
2-1/2 c. sugar
15-oz. can pumpkin, divided
1 t. cinnamon or pumpkin pie spice
7-oz. jar marshmallow creme
2 T. butter
6-oz. pkg. white chocolate chips
1 t. vanilla extract

Bring milk and sugar to a boil in a saucepan over medium heat. Stir with a wooden spoon. Mix in 3/4 of the can of pumpkin, reserving the rest for another recipe; stir in spice. Return to a boil; add marshmallow creme and butter and bring to a rolling boil. Boil, stirring often, for 18 minutes. Remove from heat. Add chocolate chips and vanilla; stir until creamy. Line a 9"x9" baking pan with plastic wrap; pour into prepared pan and let cool. Cut into squares.

Host a family reunion this fall...the weather is almost always picture-perfect!

Sweet Potato Cake

Makes 12 servings

2-1/4 c. cake flour
1 T. baking powder
1/2 t. baking soda
1/2 t. salt
1-1/2 t. cinnamon
1/2 t. allspice
1/2 t. ground ginger
3/4 c. buttermilk
3/4 c. mashed sweet potatoes
1/2 c. golden raisins
1/2 c. butter
2 eggs
1 c. brown sugar, packed
1 c. sugar
16-oz. container buttercream frosting

Mix together flour, baking powder, baking soda, salt and spices in a medium bowl; set aside. Mix together buttermilk, sweet potatoes and raisins in a small bowl; set aside. In a large bowl, beat butter until light and fluffy; add eggs one at a time, mixing thoroughly after each. Gradually add brown sugar and sugar, beating until fluffy. Add flour mixture alternately with buttermilk mixture, stirring just until smooth after each addition. Pour batter into two, greased 9" round cake pans. Bake at 350 degrees for 30 minutes, or until cake tests done. Cool; remove layers from pans and assemble with frosting.

Scoops of ice cream are a yummy garnish for warm autumn pies. Serve them in a snap...simply scoop ahead of time into paper muffin liners and freeze on a baking sheet.

Apple Crunch Pie

Makes 6 to 8 servings

2/3 c. sugar
1/4 c. all-purpose flour
1/2 t. nutmeg
1/2 t. cinnamon
1/8 t. salt
5 Granny Smith apples, cored, peeled and sliced
9-inch pie crust
Optional: 1/2 c. cranberries
Garnish: cinnamon-sugar

Whisk sugar, flour, nutmeg, cinnamon and salt in a large bowl. Stir in apples and cranberries, if using; spoon into pie crust. Top with Crumb Topping; sprinkle with cinnamon-sugar. Bake at 425 degrees for 50 minutes; sprinkle with additional cinnamon-sugar.

Crumb Topping:

1 c. all-purpose flour
1/2 c. brown sugar, packed
1/4 c. butter, chilled

Mix ingredients together until crumbly.

Nestle a warm pie or cake inside a red and orange berry wreath...
it'll be a perfect harvest welcome wreath long
after the dessert is gone!

Fresh Apple Cake

Makes 12 to 15 servings

5 baking apples, cored, peeled and sliced
2 t. cinnamon
2-1/2 c. plus 5 T. sugar, divided
3 c. all-purpose flour
1/2 t. salt
4 eggs
1 c. oil
2 t. vanilla extract
1/3 c. orange juice
1-1/2 t. baking powder
1-1/2 t. baking soda

Toss apples with cinnamon and 5 tablespoons sugar; set aside. Mix remaining ingredients together; blend well. Pour 1/3 into a greased and floured 10" tube pan; layer with one half of the apples. Repeat layers; pour remaining batter on top. Bake at 350 degrees for 1-1/2 to 1-3/4 hours or until a toothpick inserted in the center removes clean. Cool on a wire rack for 10 minutes; invert tube pan and remove to cool completely. Frost with Brown Sugar Icing.

Brown Sugar Icing:

1/2 c. shortening
1 c. brown sugar, packed
1/4 c. milk
2 c. powdered sugar

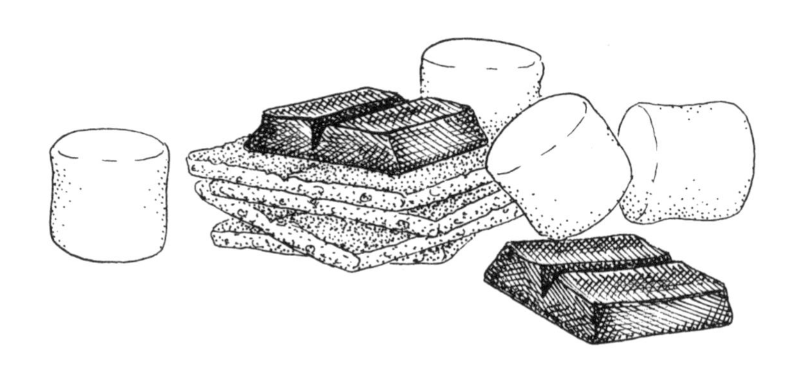

A fireside cookout before or after a hometown football game is a terrific idea on a chilly autumn night.

Skillet S'mores

Makes 10 servings

1 T. butter
10-oz. pkg. mini marshmallows
2 sleeves graham crackers, crushed
2 1-12 oz. chocolate candy bars, broken into pieces

Melt butter in a cast-iron skillet over slow, red campfire embers. Sprinkle in marshmallows; stir until completely melted. Remove from fire; stir in graham crackers and chocolate. Press into pan with back of a spoon. Allow to cool completely; cut into wedges.

Look for vintage pie plates at the flea market...filled with votives and ornamental gourds, they'll add a warm glow on a table, cupboard or pie safe.

Walnut Raisin Pie

Makes 6 to 8 servings

3 eggs, beaten
2/3 c. sugar
1/2 t. salt
1/2 t. cinnamon
1/2 t. nutmeg
1/2 t. ground cloves
1 c. corn syrup
1/3 c. butter, melted
1 c. walnuts, coarsely chopped
2 c. raisins
9-inch pie crust

Beat together eggs, sugar, salt, spices, corn syrup and butter until well mixed. Stir in walnuts and raisins; pour into pie crust. Bake at 375 degrees for 40 to 50 minutes, until set.

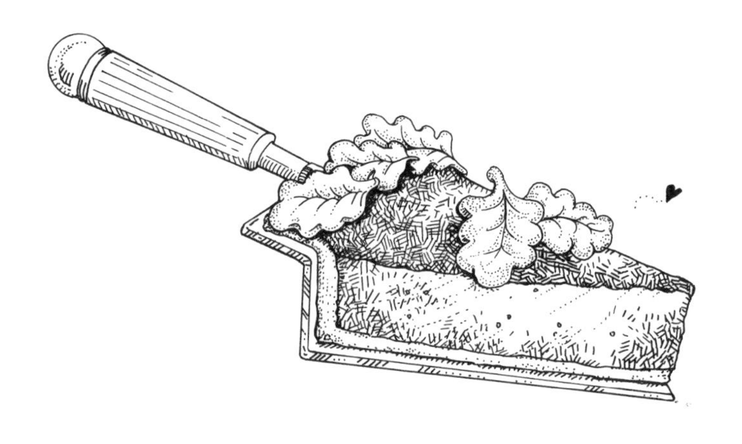

Roll out extra pie crust dough, cut with leaf-shaped mini cookie cutters and press onto the top crust before baking. What a fun pie topper!

Slow-Cooker Apple Pie

Makes 6 to 8 serving

- 8 tart apples, cored, peeled and sliced
- 1-1/4 t. cinnamon
- 1/4 t. allspice
- 1/4 t. nutmeg
- 3/4 c. milk
- 2 T. butter, softened
- 3/4 c. sugar
- 2 eggs
- 1 t. vanilla extract
- 1-1/2 c. biscuit baking mix, divided
- 1/3 c. brown sugar, packed
- 3 T. chilled butter

Toss apples with cinnamon, allspice and nutmeg. Place in a lightly greased slow cooker. Combine milk, softened butter, sugar, eggs, vanilla and 1/2 cup biscuit baking mix; spoon over apples. Combine remaining biscuit baking mix and brown sugar; cut in chilled butter until crumbly. Sprinkle over mixture in slow cooker; do not stir. Cover and cook on low setting 6 to 7 hours or until apples are tender.

Decorate a grapevine garland to wind around the front door. Garland can be found at craft stores...use orange or yellow raffia to tie on gourds, mini Indian corn and dried seed pods. It'll look wonderful all autumn long.

Haystacks

Makes 18 servings

1-1/2 c. chow mein noodles
1 c. butterscotch chips
1/2 c. peanut butter chips
1 T. shortening

Place chow mein noodles in a large mixing bowl; set aside. Melt chips and shortening together in a double boiler; stir until smooth. Pour over noodles; stir to coat. Drop by tablespoonfuls onto wax paper; set aside until firm. Store in an airtight container in the refrigerator.

Use a drill with a 1/2-inch bit to drill holes into a hollowed-out pumpkin. Fill each pumpkin with a strand of battery-operated tiny white lights for a twinkling glow.

Cocoa Brownies

Makes 1-1/2 to 2 dozen

1 c. sugar
2/3 c. all-purpose flour
1/2 c. baking cocoa
1/2 t. baking powder
1/2 c. margarine, melted
1 t. vanilla extract
2 eggs
3/4 c. semi-sweet chocolate chips

Combine sugar, flour, baking cocoa and baking powder; add margarine, vanilla and eggs. Spread in a greased 9"x9" baking pan; sprinkle with chocolate chips. Bake at 350 degrees for 20 to 25 minutes. Cut into squares.

INDEX

INDEX

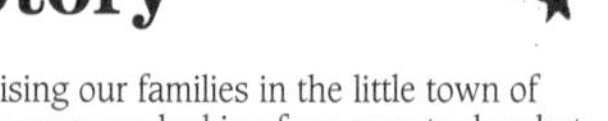

Our Story

Back in 1984, we were next-door neighbors raising our families in the little town of Delaware, Ohio. Two moms with small children, we were looking for a way to do what we loved and stay home with the kids too. We had always shared a love of home cooking and making memories with family & friends and so, after many a conversation over the backyard fence, **Gooseberry Patch** was born.

We put together our first catalog at our kitchen tables, enlisting the help of our loved ones wherever we could. From that very first mailing, we found an immediate connection with many of our customers and it wasn't long before we began receiving letters, photos and recipes from these new friends. In 1992, we put together our very first cookbook, compiled from hundreds of these recipes and, the rest, as they say, is history.

Hard to believe it's been over 25 years since those kitchen-table days! From that original little **Gooseberry Patch** family, we've grown to include an amazing group of creative folks who love cooking, decorating and creating as much as we do. Today, we're best known for our homestyle, family-friendly cookbooks, now recognized as national bestsellers.

One thing's for sure, we couldn't have done it without our friends all across the country. Each year, we're honored to turn thousands of your recipes into our collectible cookbooks. Our hope is that each book captures the stories and heart of all of you who have shared with us. Whether you've been with us since the beginning or are just discovering us, welcome to the **Gooseberry Patch** family!

Vickie & JoAnn

Visit our website anytime

www.gooseberrypatch.com

1·800·854·6673